Houghton Mifflin

Reading

Wonders

Senior Authors
J. David Cooper
John J. Pikulski

Authors
David J. Chard
Gilbert Garcia
Claude Goldenberg
Phyllis Hunter
Marjorie Y. Lipson
Shane Templeton
Sheila Valencia
MaryEllen Vogt

Consultants
Linda H. Butler
Linnea C. Ehri
Carla Ford

HOUGHTON MIFFLIN   BOSTON

Acknowledgments begin on page 236.

Printed in the U.S.A.

ISBN: 0-618-61935-6

2 3 4 5 6 7 8 9 10 DOW 11 10 09 08 07 06

Wonders

Special Friends

4

Special Friends

Focus on *Genre*

FOLKTALES

We Can Do It!

We Can Do It!

Special Friends

The New Girl

I can feel
we're much the same,
though I don't
know your name.

What friends
we're going to be
when I know you
and you know me!

by Charlotte Zolotow

When I Am Old with You
Story by ANGELA JOHNSON Pictures by DAVID SOMAN

When I Am Old with You

Genre **Realistic Fiction**

My Grandaddy

Read about the special things a grandfather and grandchild do in the next story.

Words to Know

around	though
dance	by
else	my
open	try
talk	cry
ever	any
ocean	Grandaddy

14

Practice Sentences

1. My Grandaddy likes to take walks by the ocean.
2. He likes to dance when no one else is around.
3. We try to talk every day.
4. Sometimes we're too busy to talk, though.
5. When I miss him, I start to cry.
6. Any day now, I will open my door and there he will be.
7. He is the best Grandaddy ever!

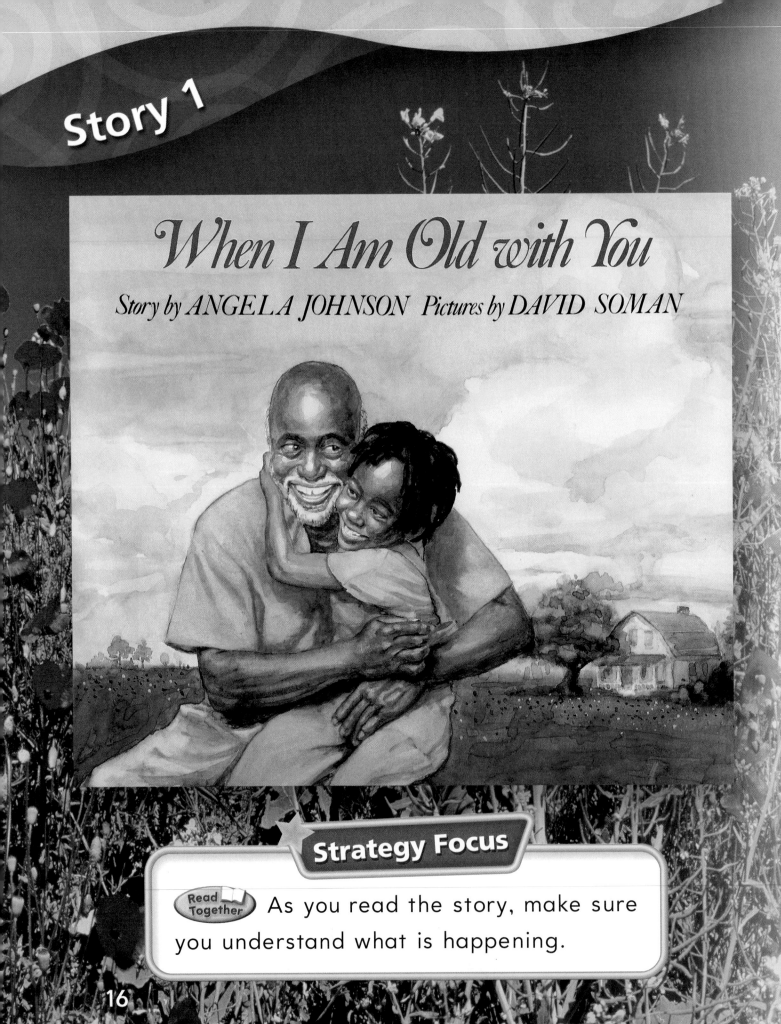

When I Am Old with You

Story by ANGELA JOHNSON   Pictures by DAVID SOMAN

Strategy Focus

Read Together   As you read the story, make sure you understand what is happening.

When I am old with you, Grandaddy,
I will sit in a big rocking chair beside
you and talk about everything.

An old dog will sit by my feet,
and I will swat flies all afternoon.

We'll go fishing too,
Grandaddy, down by that old pond
with the flat rocks all around.

We can fish beside the pond
or take that old canoe out.

We'll eat out of the picnic basket
all day and we won't catch any fish . . .
. . . but that's all right, Grandaddy.

When I am old with you, Grandaddy,
we will play cards all day underneath that
old tree by the road.

We'll drink cool water from a jug
and wave at all the cars that go by.

24

We'll play cards till the
lightning bugs shine in the trees . . .

. . . and we won't mind that we
forgot to keep score, Grandaddy.

25

When I am old with you, Grandaddy, we
will open up that old cedar chest and try on all
the old clothes that your grandaddy left you.

We can look at the old
pictures and try to imagine
the people in them.
    It might make us cry . . .
but that's O.K.

In the mornings, Grandaddy, we will
cook bacon for breakfast and that's all.

We can eat it on the porch too.

In the evening we can roast corn on a big fire and invite everyone we know to come over and eat it. They'll all dance, play cards, and talk about everything.

When I am old with you, Grandaddy,
we can take a trip to the ocean.

Have you ever seen the ocean,
Grandaddy?

We'll walk on the hot sand
and throw rocks at the waves.

We can wear big hats in the
afternoon like everyone else . . .
. . . and we'll sit in the water when
the day gets cool.

When our trip is over we will
follow the ocean as far as we can,
so we'll never forget it.

When I am old with you, Grandaddy,
we will get on the tractor and ride through
the fields of grass.

We will see the trees in the distance
and remember when this field was a forest.

We won't be sad though.

Grandaddy, when I am old with
you we will take long walks and speak
to all the people who walk by us.

We'll know them all, Grandaddy,
and they'll know us.

At the end of our walk, when we're tired,
Grandaddy, I will sit in a big rocking chair . . .
beside you.

Meet the Author and the Illustrator

Angela Johnson started writing in a diary when she was nine. Her advice for writers is to write your thoughts down so you can save them for later.

David Soman has always loved to draw and paint. When he was young, he liked to doodle. David Soman teaches art in New York City.

Internet

To find out more about Angela Johnson and David Soman, visit Education Place.

www.eduplace.com/kids

Read Together

When I Am Old with You
Story by ANGELA JOHNSON   Pictures by DAVID SOMAN

Think About the Story

1. Why do you think the grandchild and grandfather spend so much time together?

2. Do you think the grandchild will have happy memories of Grandaddy? Why?

3. What makes Grandaddy a special friend?

4. Which of the things in the story would you like to do with a friend? Why?

Internet

Post a Review

What did you think of this story?
Post your review at Education Place.

www.eduplace.com/kids

Listening and Speaking

Let's Talk

Work with a partner. Choose a scene from the story. Act out a conversation that might happen between the grandchild and Grandaddy.

Math

Take a Poll

In a group, take a poll about favorite activities from the story. Make a graph to show how many votes each activity gets.

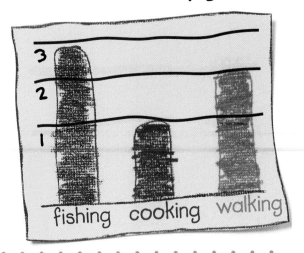

Expressing

Write a Message

Write a message to a special friend. Tell about something you could do together.

Tips
- **Think about things you both enjoy.**
- **Write clearly.**

Read Together

Inventions Then and Now

Bicycles

Today bicycles look like this.

In the past, bicycles didn't give a very smooth ride. Some people called these early bicycles boneshakers!

Here are some of the telephones we use today. We can call people around the world.

The first telephone call was made from one room to another in the same building. Some early phones were made of wood and hung on walls.

Clocks

Today clocks can
look like these.

Before clocks were
invented, some people
used hourglasses. It takes
one hour for the sand to
run from the top bulb to
the bottom bulb.

Past Inventions

Here are some other inventions from long ago. How are they different from the ones we use today?

lawn mower

phonograph

camera

roller skates

A Friendly Letter

A friendly letter tells a special friend about what you are doing. Use this student's writing as a model when you write a friendly letter of your own.

A friendly letter has the **date** and a **greeting**.

The main part of the letter is the **body**.

April 21, 2003

Dear Jennie,

You are my best friend. I like you because you help me with my school work and you play with me.

Jennie →   ← me

My favorite thing is when we pick flowers together. I am always happy to see you.

Your friend,
Marissa

Meet the Author

Marissa S.
Grade: one
State: Delaware
Hobbies: reading, writing, collecting rings
What she'd like to be when she grows up: a kindergarten teacher

49

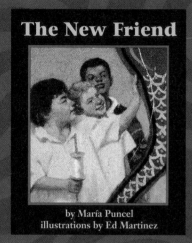

The New Friend

by María Puncel
illustrations by Ed Martinez

The New Friend

Genre   **Realistic Fiction**

A New Family

In the next story, you'll read about a new friend who moves to the neighborhood.

Words to Know

after	brushes
before	wishes
school	boxes
pretty	families
done	unloaded
buy	unpack
off	repaid
wash	

Practice Sentences

1. A new family came to buy the house next to our school.

2. They started to wash inside the house with brushes and mops.

3. They unloaded boxes off a truck and started to unpack.

4. They were done in no time.

5. After lunch, I took over a cake.

6. I gave them my best wishes.

7. Before long, the new family repaid us with some pretty flowers.

8. I hope our families will be friends!

51

Meet the Author and the Illustrator

María Puncel wrote this story in Spanish. She lives in Spain. She first told stories to her six younger brothers and sisters. Now she writes books and TV shows.

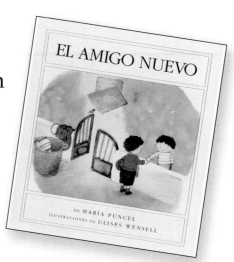

EL AMIGO NUEVO

DE MARÍA PUNCEL
ILUSTRACIONES DE ULISES WENSELL

Ed Martinez thinks it's exciting to paint outdoors. He lives in the country in a house that's three hundred years old!

Internet

Go to Education Place to find out more about María Puncel and Ed Martinez.

www.eduplace.com/kids

The New Friend

by María Puncel
illustrations by Ed Martinez

Strategy Focus

Read Together   After you read the story, think about whether the author did a good job of telling the story.

53

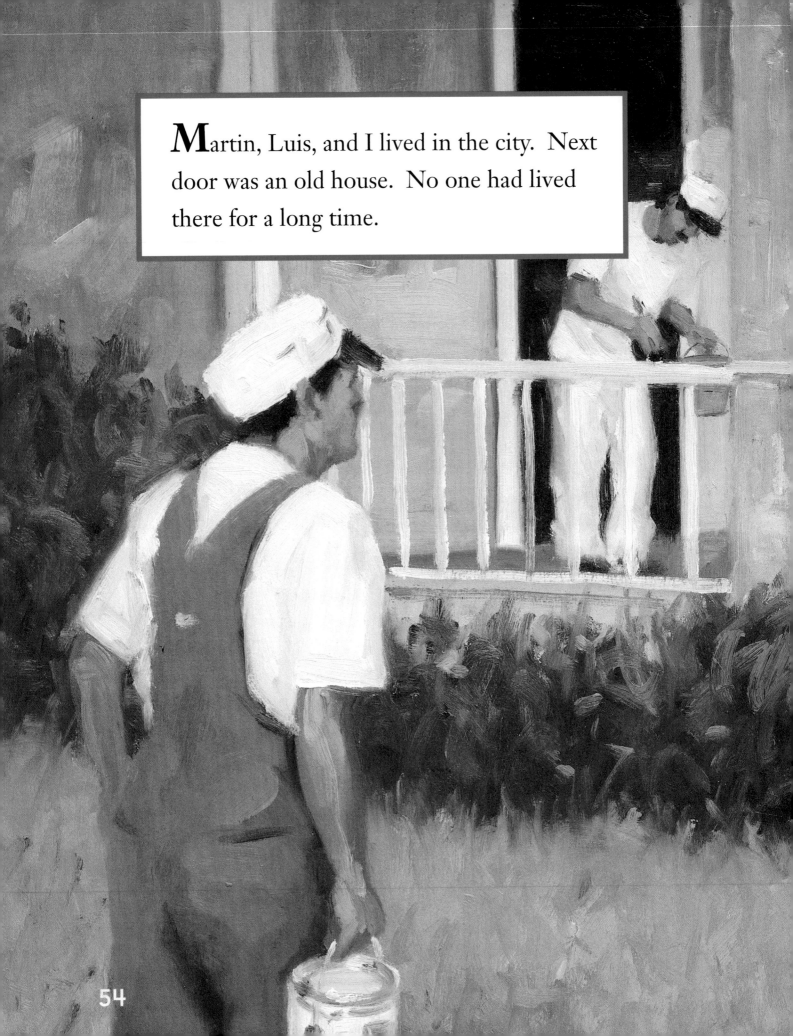

Martin, Luis, and I lived in the city. Next door was an old house. No one had lived there for a long time.

54

One day a work crew came with pails and brushes. They started to wash and paint the empty house.

55

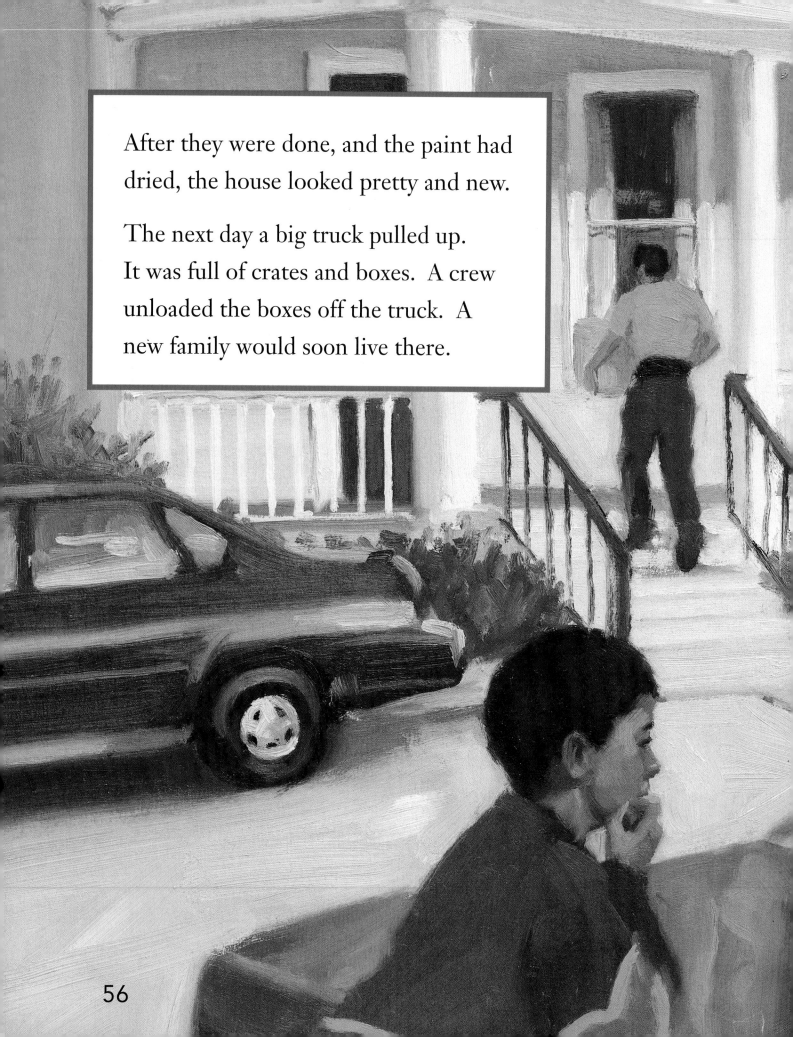

After they were done, and the paint had dried, the house looked pretty and new.

The next day a big truck pulled up. It was full of crates and boxes. A crew unloaded the boxes off the truck. A new family would soon live there.

56

Today Luis went over to the house next door.
He met a boy called Makoto. Then we all
met Makoto. Makoto was seven years old —
just like us.

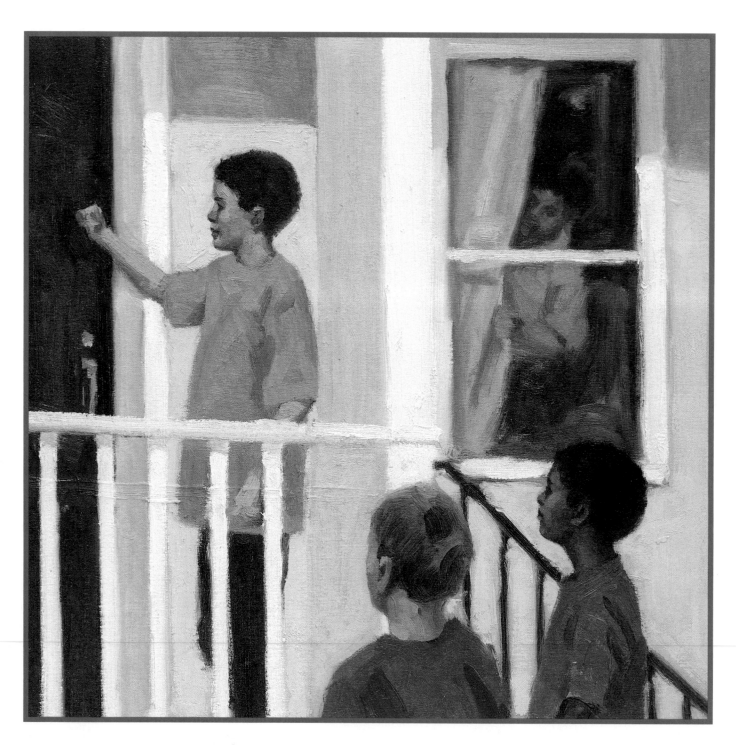

Before long, we found out that Makoto played
soccer. He could keep running and running.
He was good at learning things, too. He
learned all of our names by the end of the game.

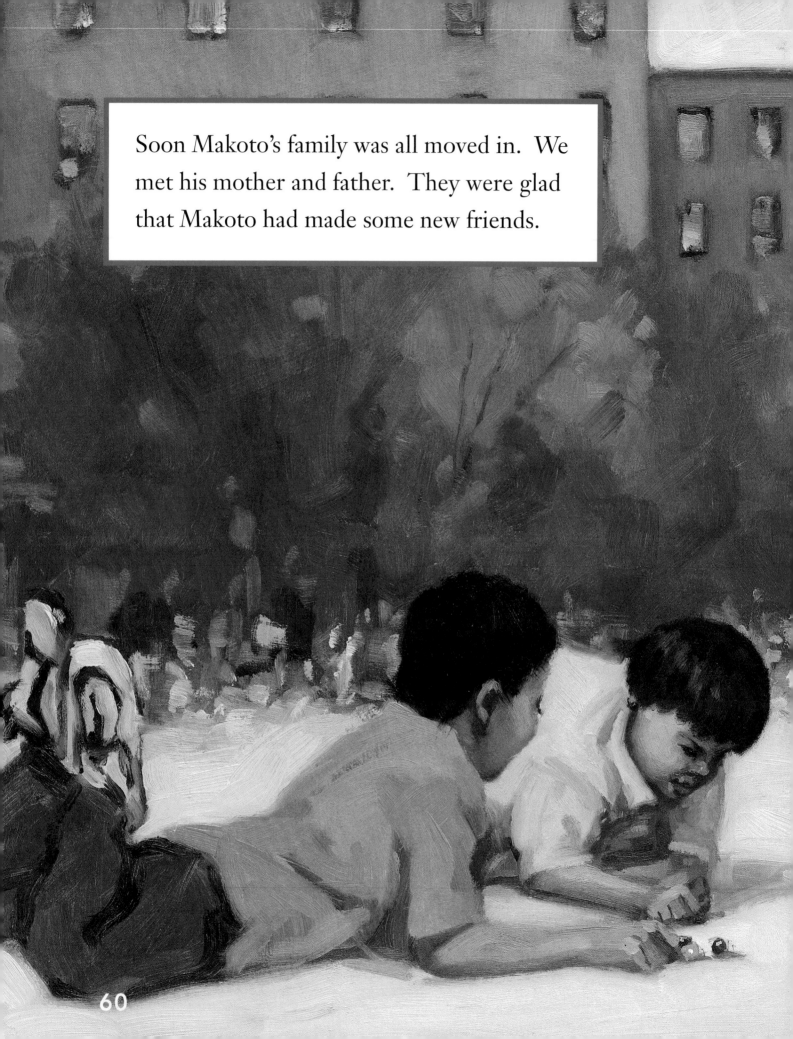

Soon Makoto's family was all moved in. We met his mother and father. They were glad that Makoto had made some new friends.

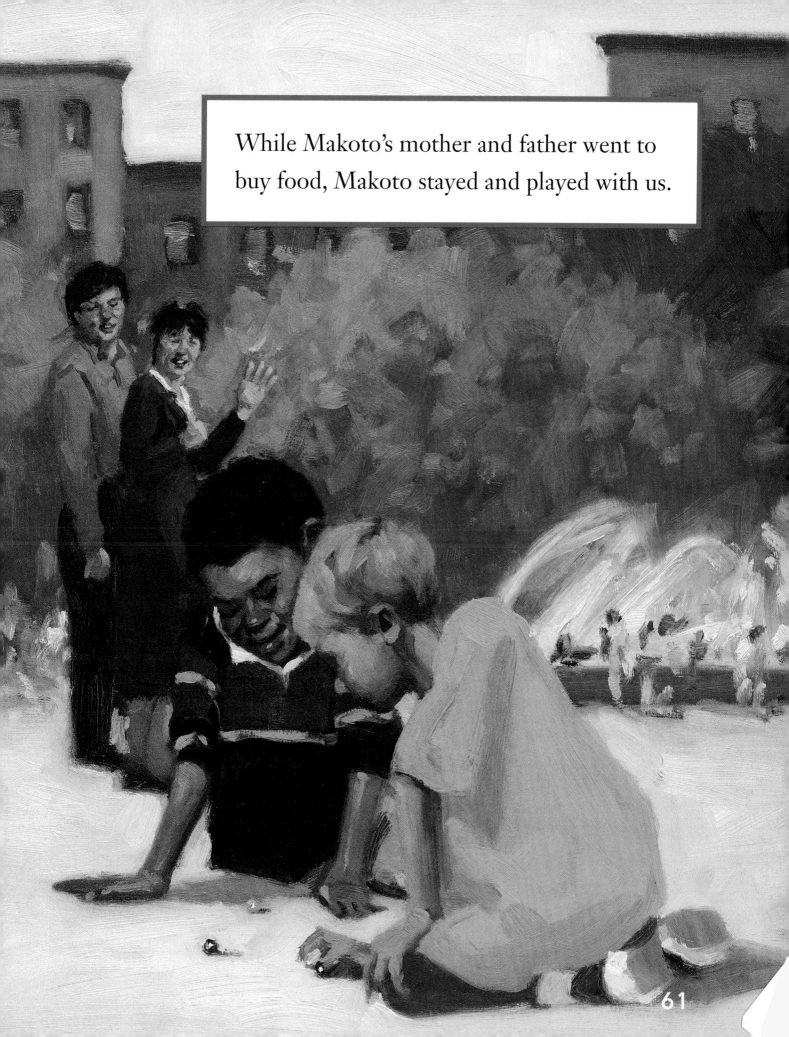

While Makoto's mother and father went to buy food, Makoto stayed and played with us.

When Makoto's mother and father rejoined
us, Martin, Makoto, and I helped them carry
the bags into the house.

Makoto said he would show us around
his house. Then we went up to look at
Makoto's room.

Makoto still had a lot of boxes to unpack.
He had some nice toys and kites. He
said that on the next windy day, we could
bring his kites outside and fly them. He
said I could fly a kite by myself.

Then we went outside to look at Makoto's
pictures from Japan. He had them in a
green book.

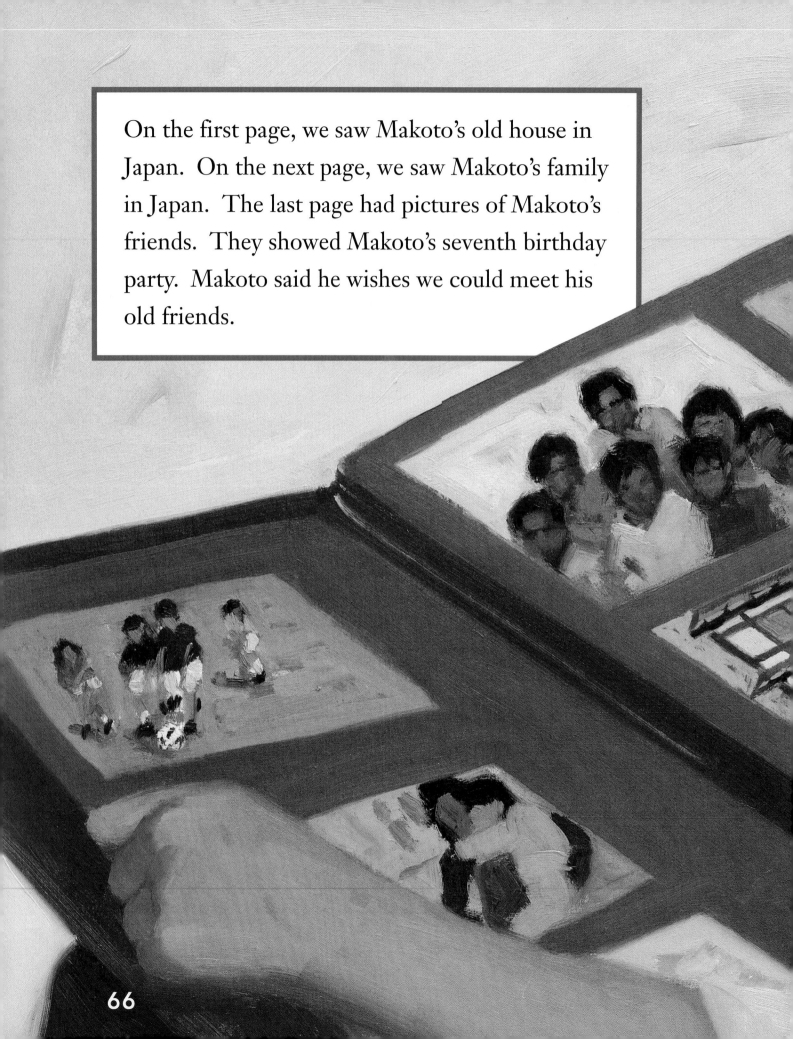

On the first page, we saw Makoto's old house in Japan. On the next page, we saw Makoto's family in Japan. The last page had pictures of Makoto's friends. They showed Makoto's seventh birthday party. Makoto said he wishes we could meet his old friends.

At the end of the day, Makoto's mother and
father repaid us for helping — with cookies!
We said "please" and "thank you" and ate up.

Makoto's father said he had a new job in the
city. Makoto would be going to our school.
We were all glad about that!

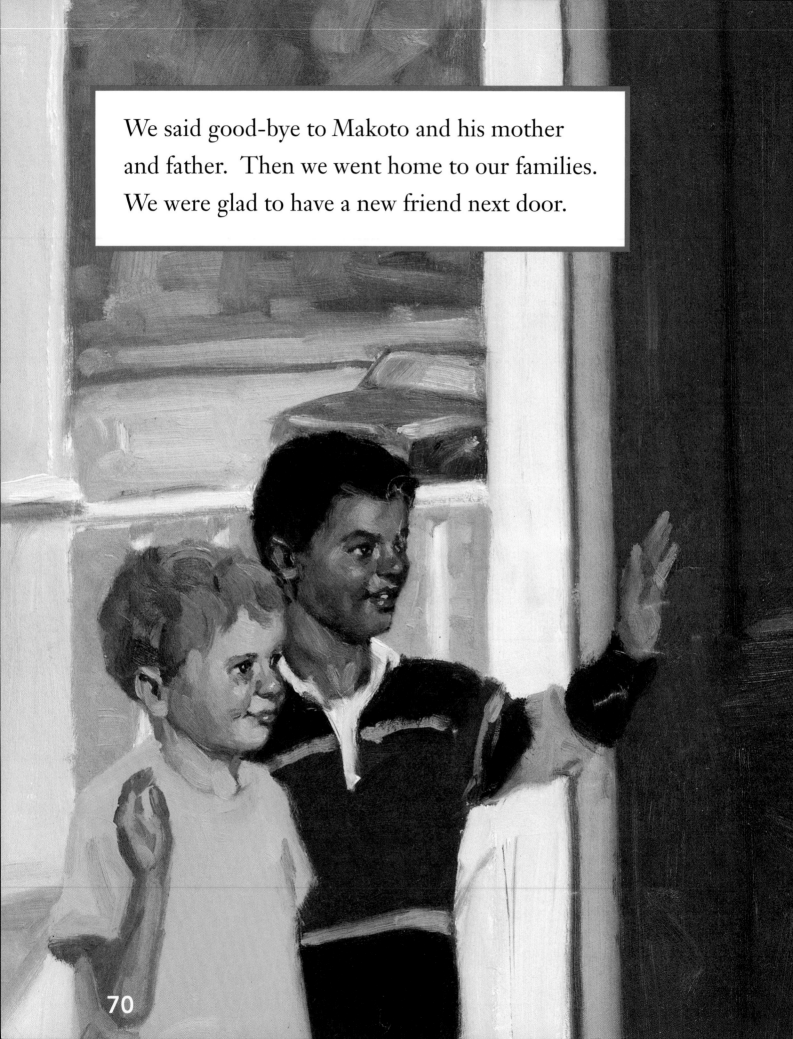

We said good-bye to Makoto and his mother and father. Then we went home to our families. We were glad to have a new friend next door.

The New Friend

by María Puncel
illustrations by Ed Martinez

Think About the Story

1. How do you think the children felt about Makoto moving to their neighborhood?

2. How do you think Makoto felt about moving?

3. Do you think Makoto will like his new home? Why?

4. What would you do to make a new neighbor feel welcome?

Internet

Build a Story

Visit Education Place to put the story events in the order in which they happened.

www.eduplace.com/kids

Stay Healthy

Make a book about how
to stay healthy. Write a
sentence on each page
and draw a picture to
go with it.

Write an Invitation

Think of something you
would like to do with a
friend. Then send an
invitation to your friend.

Tips

- **Begin with a greeting.**
- **Tell what you are inviting
  your friend to do.**
- **Include the date, time,
  and place.**

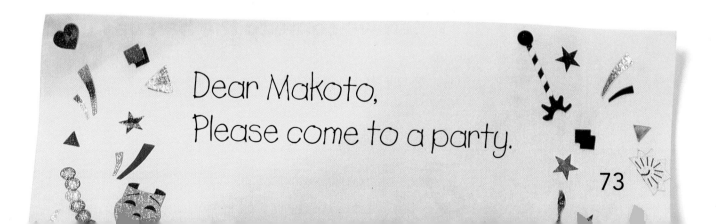

Dear Makoto,
Please come to a party.

73

Poetry
Link

Read
Together

Genre

Poetry

Skill: How to Read a Poem

- **Read** the poem aloud.

- **Listen** for the beat.

- **Reread** the poem and tap the beat.

I'll walk halfway to your house

if you walk halfway to mine.

We'll decide about the other half

when we come to the halfway line.

by Charlotte Pomerantz

74

HOPE

Sometimes when I'm lonely,

Don't know why,

Keep thinkin' I won't be lonely

By and by.

by Langston Hughes

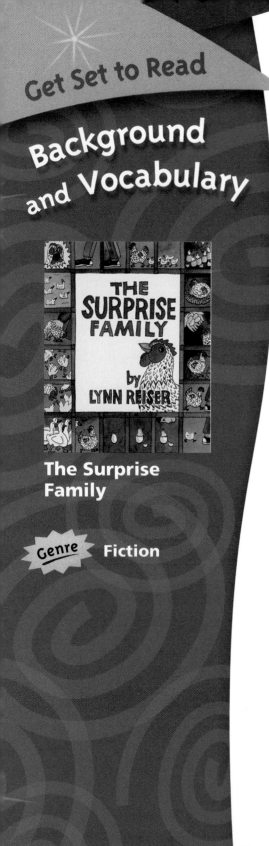

The Surprise Family

Genre **Fiction**

Baby Birds

What happens when a hen doesn't get the kind of babies she expects? Read the next story to find out.

Words to Know

only	boy
together	pointed
watched	saw
baby	hawk
edge	taught
enough	fluffy
garden	fuzzy
sharp	

76

Practice Sentences

1. A boy and his mother went out together into the garden.
2. They saw fuzzy, fluffy baby birds on the ground.
3. They watched the birds creep to the edge of the garden.
4. The mother pointed up to a hawk with a sharp beak.
5. She taught the boy that the only safe place was in the nest.
6. "That should be enough to keep the baby birds safe," the mother said.

THE
SURPRISE
FAMILY
by
LYNN REISER

Strategy Focus

Read Together   What questions do you have about this story? Read the story to find out the answers to your questions.

First there was an egg.

One day it cracked open.

A baby chick looked out.
Nobody was there.
Where was her mother?

The baby chick looked up and saw —
a boy.

Her mother was a boy!
The boy was not the kind of mother
the chick had expected, but she loved
him anyway.

She followed him
everywhere.
The boy showed his
baby chick how to find
water and food and grit
for her gizzard.

He taught her how to
hide safe inside his
jacket when a hawk flew
by or when the vacuum
cleaner came too close.

Every afternoon the boy and his baby
chick went for a walk around the garden.

At night she slept warm under the edge
of his quilt.

The baby chick grew and grew and became a little hen.

She still followed the boy everywhere, but now following the boy was not enough.
She wanted a family to follow her.

She built a nest.

The boy found a clutch of eggs.
He gave them to the little hen.

She sat and warmed the eggs, and every day she turned the eggs,

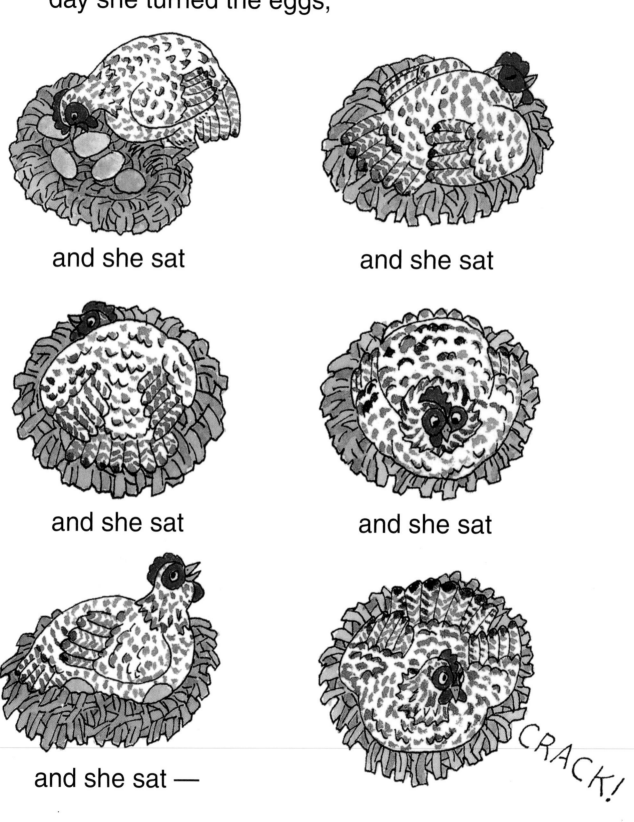

and she sat

and she sat

and she sat

and she sat

and she sat —

CRACK!

86

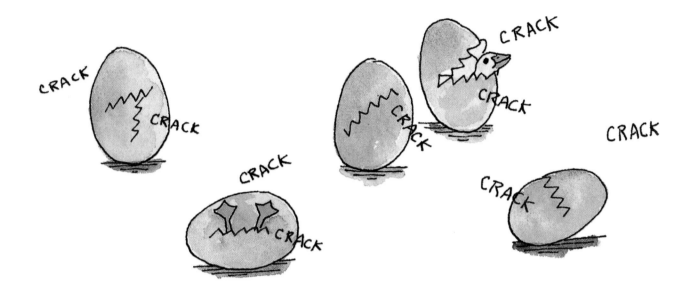

The eggs cracked open.
The babies looked out and saw
the little hen.

They followed her everywhere.
She showed them how to find water
and food and grit for their gizzards.

She taught them to run to her when she
sang a danger song and danced a danger
dance and to hide safe under her feathers.

Every afternoon the boy and the little hen and the babies went for a walk around the garden.

At night the babies slept warm under
the little hen's wings.

The little hen's family grew.
They still followed her everywhere,
but now walking around the garden
was not enough.
They wanted to walk by the pond.

So the boy and the hen took them to
walk by the pond.

They stood at the edge of the water.

They looked at the water.

They took a drink of the water.

They jumped into the water!

The little hen cried her DANGER cry —
her babies splashed.

The little hen danced her DANGER dance
— her babies swam.

The little hen held out her wings for her
babies to run under —
but they kept on swimming farther and
farther away.

The little hen ran after them, but
when her feet got wet, she stopped.
She was a chicken.
Chickens cannot swim.

The little hen's babies swam out of sight.
Only her boy was left.

Then the little hen's babies turned around,
swam back, hopped out of the water,
flapped their wings, shook their tails, and
ran to their mother hen.

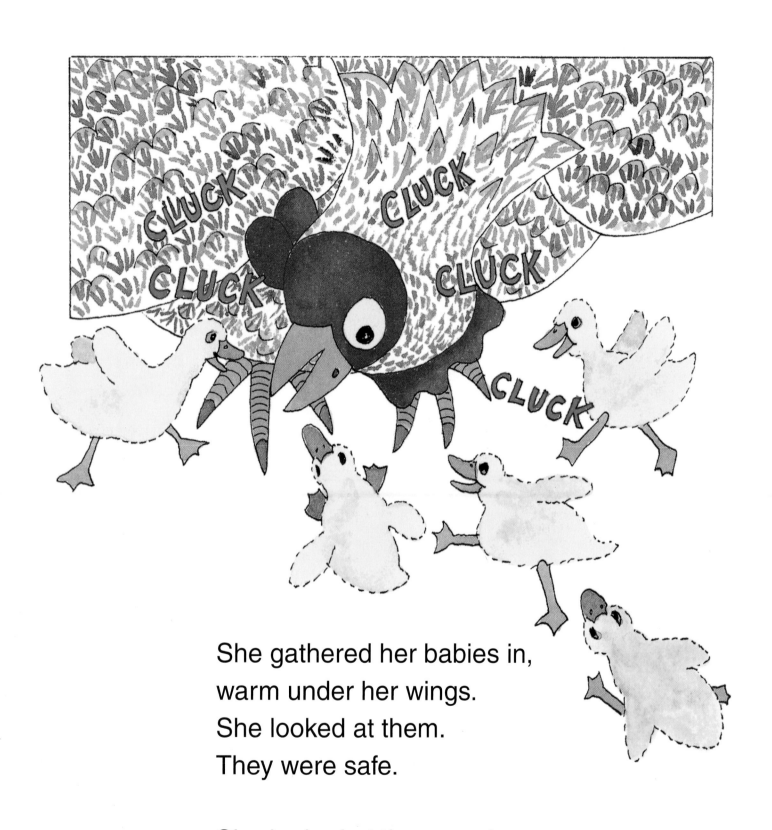

She gathered her babies in,
warm under her wings.
She looked at them.
They were safe.

She looked at them again.
Carefully.

Their beaks were not pointed like her
beak, or soft like her boy's mouth —
they were flat.

Their feet were not sharp like her feet,
or hard like her boy's shoes —
they were webbed.

Their feathers were not fluffy like her
feathers, or fuzzy like her boy's jacket —
they were waterproof.

Her babies did not look like chicks or like
boys. They looked like ducklings.

Ducklings were not the kind of family she
had expected, but she loved them anyway.

The ducklings grew and grew and became big ducks.

Some afternoons while the ducks swam in the pond, the boy walked around the garden, and the hen followed him.

Some afternoons while the ducks swam in the pond, the hen walked around the garden, and the boy followed her.

Other afternoons while the ducks swam in the pond, and the boy waded after them, the hen watched.

But every afternoon in the garden beside
the pond, after walking and swimming
and wading, there they all were, together,
under the little hen's wings.

QUACK

108

Meet the Author and Illustrator

Lynn Reiser not only writes children's books, but she is also a doctor and a professor. She thinks that all families are surprise families!

Internet

Find out more about Lynn Reiser at Education Place.

www.eduplace.com/kids

Think About the Story

1. Why do you think the story was called *The Surprise Family*?

2. How do you think the hen feels when her babies swim away in the pond?

3. Does it matter to the hen when she finds out her babies are different from her? Why?

4. What would you have done if you were the boy in the story?

Complete a Word Search

Go on a search for words from the story. Visit Education Place to print out a word search puzzle.

www.eduplace.com/kids

Viewing

Words in Art

Look back at the story. Do you notice some words in the art? Find some other books that show words in the art. Share them with the group.

Science

Chicken and Duck

Draw a chicken and a duck. Label the parts of each animal that are different. Share your picture with the class.

Write a Newspaper Article

Write an article about what happens in *The Surprise Family*. Write sentences to tell the facts and include a picture.

Tip
- **Write an interesting headline.**

News of the Day

Hen's Babies Can Swim!

111

Genre

Science Article

Skill: How to Read a Science Article

- **Read** the title of the article.

- **Read** the heading for each section.

- **Look** at the photos.

- **Predict** what you will learn.

- **Reread** if something is unclear.

Watch Them Grow

by Linda Martin

1. Hatching

A duckling pushes its way out of an egg laid by its mother.

2. Splash!

After only two days, a duckling goes for its first swim.
It loves it!

3. New feathers

This duckling is not as round as it was before. Its baby feathers are falling out. New white feathers are growing in their place.

4. Fine wings

This duckling is six weeks old. All its feathers are white and its wings are big and strong. Soon it will fly for the first time.

Eggs

Some baby animals hatch from eggs. Do you think you can guess what will hatch from these eggs? Look for their mothers on the next page.

1

2

3

4

5

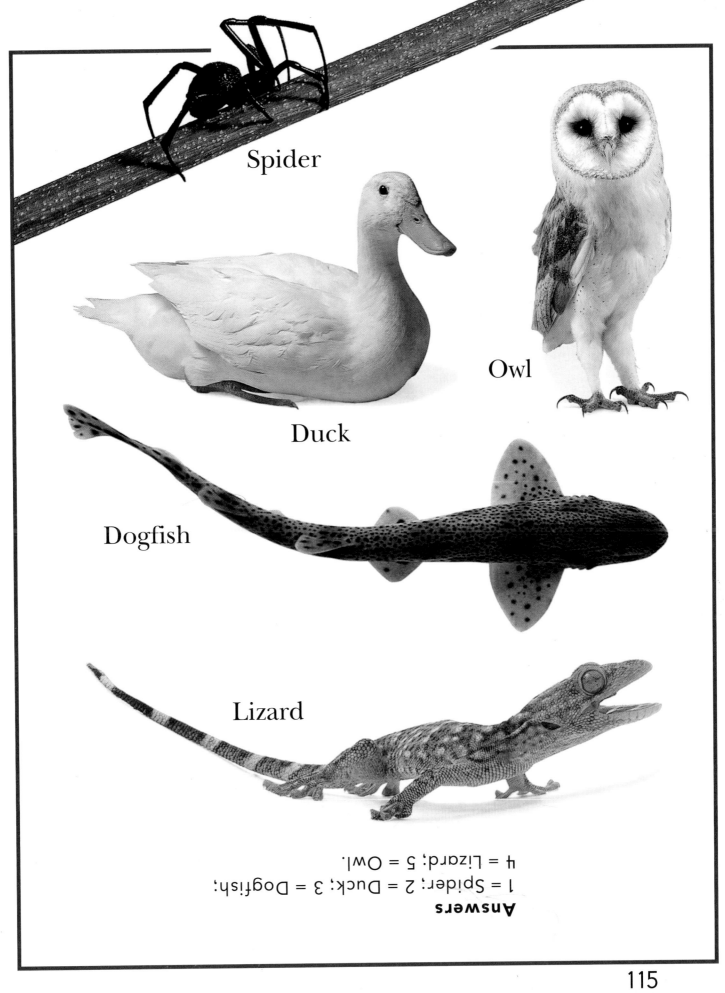

Spider

Duck

Owl

Dogfish

Lizard

Writing an Answer to a Question

Some tests ask you to write an answer to a question about something you have read. Here is a sample test for *The Surprise Family*.

In *The Surprise Family*, the hen and her babies are not alike in some ways. What are two things that are different about the hen and her babies? Write your answer.

Tips

- Read the directions carefully.
- Make sure your sentences tell about the question.
- Write on the lines.

I look for the key words that tell me what to write about. I think the key words are **different**, **hen**, and **babies**. I will write about two things that are different about the hen and her babies.

What is different about the hen and her babies? I need to look back through the story.

Now read a good answer to the test question.

The hen has a pointed beak, and the babies have round beaks. The hen has sharp feet, and the babies have webbed feet.

FOLKTALES

Focus on Genre

118

FOLKTALES

A folktale is a kind of story that people have been telling for a long, long time. Parents tell folktales to their children, who grow up and tell them to their children.

Sometimes a character learns an important lesson, as you will see in these two folktales!

CONTENTS

Focus on Genre

Sister Hen's Cool Drink

retold by Angela Shelf Medearis

One afternoon Hen went down by the
creek, looking for a cool drink.
Hen drank and drank. She did not hear
Crocodile as he came swimming up to her.

120

In a loud tone Crocodile said, "Stop
drinking from my creek, or I will eat you up!"
My, oh my! Hen ran from Crocodile as
fast as she could.

But Crocodile came slinking after her. He grabbed her tail.

"Please don't eat me, brother!" Hen said.

My, oh my! When Hen called Crocodile "brother," it made his jaws drop open. So, quick as a wink, Hen yanked her tail out and ran away. She did not stop running until she was safe in her nest.

"My, oh my!" Crocodile was thinking. "Why did Hen call me her brother?"

He slinked off the muddy bank into the
creek. Kaplunk!

Crocodile could not think why Hen
would call him "brother." He did not have
feet like Hen. Hen did not have teeth like
Crocodile.

He was still thinking about it the next day when Hen came down from her nest for a cool drink from the creek.

"Stop!" said Crocodile, slinking up next to her. "I want to ask you something."

"What is it?" Hen said. This time she was not afraid.

"Why did you call me your brother? I was thinking and thinking about it, but I do not get it," Crocodile said. "You are small and I am big. You are black and I am green. How can I be your brother?"

"Because," said Hen, "you come from an egg, and I come from an egg. So we must be family."

"Thank you," said Crocodile. "In that case, I guess I can't eat you after all."

Then Crocodile slinked off the muddy bank into the creek.

Kaplunk!

What Is in Mole's Sack?

retold by Gretchen Will Mayo

Coyote was walking along. "There is
Mole's tunnel!" said Coyote.

He went over to look.

Scritch, scrape, scrape. Mole was busy.

"Working hard, Mole?" called Coyote.

"Yup!" Mole scraped some more.

Coyote found a tree and sat down to watch Mole. Coyote thought, "I'm so smart. I can rest in the shade. No hard work for me!"

Mole ran in and out of his house. He carried a little sack on his back.

"Mole, why are you working so hard?" Coyote called. He leaned against the tree.

"Busy cleaning," answered Mole. He scraped some more.

Coyote stared at Mole's sack. "Why is
Mole carrying that sack?" Coyote wondered.
"What does he have in it?"

Coyote called out, "Mole, you must have
something good in your sack."

"Nope," said Mole.

Coyote didn't believe him. Coyote thought, "If I had something good in a sack, I would keep it just for me. I'll bet Mole doesn't want to share."

Coyote called sweetly, "Let me look in your sack."

"Nope," said Mole.

"Just a little peek," begged Coyote. "I'll just open the sack a little bit."

"Don't," Mole said.

Coyote jumped up. He walked over to Mole. "I know. You want to keep the sack just for you."

"Nope," answered Mole.

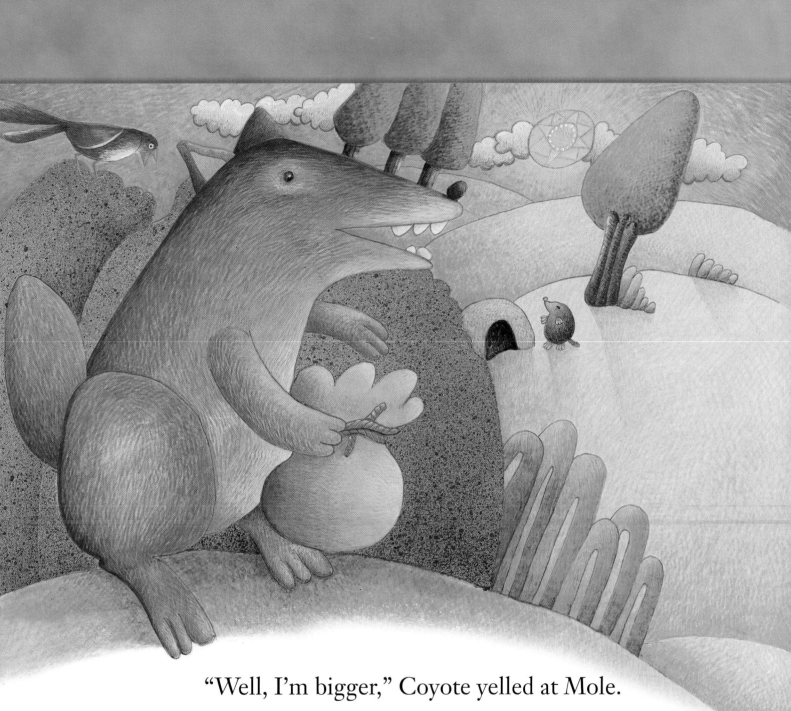

"Well, I'm bigger," Coyote yelled at Mole. "You won't let me take a look, so I'll take the whole thing!"

And he did. Coyote grabbed Mole's sack and ran back down the road. He hid behind a rock. He smiled a little smile. Then he opened the sack.

"Eeeeeeeeee, no!" he cried. Zit-zit-zit-zit-zit! Out leaped a crowd of fleas. They jumped all over Coyote.

"Go away!" Coyote yelled. "Go away!" He slap-slap-slapped. He hopped. He rolled in the dirt. But the fleas hung on to Coyote. They liked his ears. They liked his back. They liked this big Coyote.

Coyote ran back to Mole's tunnel. "Mole!" he cried. "Take back your fleas. Take them back!"

But Mole ran away. He ran into his house and would not come out.

Coyote can't rest in the shade now. Scratch! Scratch! Scratch! Coyote is busy all the time. Scratching fleas is hard work.

Think About the

Read Together

FOLKTALES

1. Mole and Hen each play tricks to teach a lesson. What else could they do besides playing tricks?

2. Which character do you think is the smartest? Why?

3. What advice would you give to Coyote?

4. Which folktale would you like to tell to someone else? Why?

Internet

Take an Online Quiz

What do you know about folktales? Take an online quiz. See what you have learned!

www.eduplace.com/kids

Write a Folktale

Would you like to write your own folktale? Here are some steps to follow:

1. Think of interesting characters for your folktale.
2. Decide if one character is going to learn a lesson.
3. Plan the order of events.
4. Think about adding dialogue and a funny twist at the end of your folktale.

Have a class folktale festival. Everyone can read aloud his or her folktale.

Theme 10

We Can Do It!

A Year Later

Last summer I couldn't swim at all;

I couldn't even float;

I had to use a rubber tube

Or hang on to a boat;

I had to sit on shore

While everybody swam;

But now it's this summer

And I can!

by Mary Ann Hoberman

Background and Vocabulary

Two Greedy Bears

 Genre **Fantasy**

Thirsty Bears

Read the next story to find out what happens to two bear cubs who want the same piece of cheese. When a sly fox comes by, the bears learn a lesson!

Words to Know

began	burst
laugh	turning
sure	more
head	morning
divide	her
second	other
break	water
thirsty	better
thirstier	

Practice Sentences

1. One bear was thirsty.
2. The other bear was thirstier.
3. The second bear drank more and more water.
4. The first bear began to laugh.
5. "You are going to burst!" she said.
6. "You'd better stop drinking!"
7. Turning her head, the second bear said, "I am hungry."
8. "We can divide this food if we break it in two."
9. "Sure," said the first bear.
10. "We can do that in the morning."

Meet the Author

When she was young, **Mirra Ginsburg**'s parents taught her to love books. Now she is an author and has written more than 30 books. Some of her favorite things are folktales, poetry, and very old music.

Internet

Learn more about Mirra Ginsburg at Education Place.

www.eduplace.com/kids

142

Two Greedy Bears

Adapted from a Hungarian Folk Tale

By Mirra Ginsburg

Pictures by
Jose Aruego & Ariane Dewey

Strategy Focus

Read Together   What do you think two greedy
bear cubs will do when they find one piece
of cheese? Read the story to find out.

Two bear cubs went out to see the world.
They walked and walked, till they came to a brook.
"I'm thirsty," said one.
"I'm thirstier," said the other.

They put their heads down to the water and drank.
"You had more," cried one, and drank some more.
"Now you had more," cried the other, and drank some more.

And so they drank and drank, and their stomachs got bigger and bigger, till a frog peeked out of the water and laughed.

"Look at those pot-bellied bear cubs!
If they drink any more they'll burst!"

The bear cubs sat down on the grass and looked at their stomachs.

"I have a stomach ache," one cried.
"I have a bigger one," cried the other.
They cried and cried, till they fell asleep.

In the morning they woke up feeling better
and continued their journey.
"I am hungry," said one.
"I am hungrier," said the other.

And suddenly they saw a big round cheese
lying by the roadside. They wanted to
divide it. But they did not know how to
break it into equal parts. Each was afraid the
other would get the bigger piece.

152

They argued, and they growled, and they began to fight, till a fox came by.

"What are you arguing about?" the sly one asked the bear cubs.

"We don't know how to divide the cheese so that we'll both get equal parts."

"That's easy," she said. "I'll help you."

154

She took the cheese and broke it in two.
But she made sure that one piece was bigger
than the other, and the bear cubs cried,
"That one is bigger!"

"Don't worry. I know what to do." And she took a big bite out of the larger piece. "Now that one's bigger!"

"Have patience!" And she took a bite out of
the second piece.
"Now this one's bigger!"

159

"Wait, wait," the fox said with her mouth full of cheese. "In just a moment they'll be equal." She took another bite, and then another.

160

And the bear cubs kept turning their black
noses from the bigger piece to the smaller
one, from the smaller one to the bigger one.
"Now this one's bigger!"
"Now that one's bigger!"

And the fox kept on dividing and dividing
the cheese, till she could eat no more.
"And now, good appetite to you, my friends!"
She flicked her tail and stalked away.

By then all that was left of the big round
cheese were two tiny crumbs.
But they were equal!

Meet the Illustrators

Jose Aruego and Ariane Dewey

Jose Aruego and Ariane Dewey are a team. They have worked together on more than 65 books. Jose Aruego draws the lines, and Ariane Dewey fills them in with color.

Internet

Learn more about Jose Aruego and Ariane Dewey at Education Place.

www.eduplace.com/kids

Think About the Story

1. What did the two bears learn about solving problems?

2. What might the bears have done if the fox had not come by?

3. What would you do if you and a friend found one thing that you both wanted?

4. What advice would you give to the two greedy bears?

Post a Review

Write a review of *Two Greedy Bears*. Post your review at Education Place.

www.eduplace.com/kids

Divide It Up

1. Work with a partner. Draw a picture of something to share. Cut it out.

2. Decide how to divide your picture into two equal parts.

3. Cut the picture in two. Did you each get an equal piece?

Explaining

Write Sentences

Write some sentences to explain to a friend why they should share something with you.

Tips

- Write the sentences as if you were speaking them.
- Use strong words that will convince your friend.

Fraction Action

by Loreen Leedy

One morning, Miss Prime turned off all the lights in the classroom.

Watch how to draw a fraction.

Start with a WHOLE shape.

Then make it into two equal parts.

Each part is called ONE HALF.

169

170

171

Read Together

Instructions

The reason for writing instructions is to tell others how to do or make something. Use this student's writing as a model when you write your own instructions.

How to Make a Bed

Do you want your bed to be messy or not? If you want your bed nice, then pay attention to my directions. First, you need the following materials:

1. Bed
2. Sheets
3. Pillow
4. Pillowcase
5. Blanket

It's important to list **materials** the reader will need.

172

Now follow the instructions in this order. First, put the sheets on the bed. (Hint, take the sheets and spread them out first.) Next, put the blankets on the bed. Then put the pillow on the bed. Fluff it. Finally, check it to see if the bed is messy or not.

Follow my directions, and your bed will look neat, too.

Present your steps in a clear **order**.

Use **time-order words** to show the reader what to do first, next, and last.

Meet the Author

Sara C.
Grade: one
State: Kentucky
Hobbies: reading, playing outdoors
What she'd like to be when she grows up: a veterinarian

Fireflies for Nathan

Genre Realistic Fiction

A Jar of Fireflies

In this story, you will read about a boy who spends time with his grandparents. They catch fireflies in a jar just like the boy's father did when he was six.

Words to Know

above	minute
against	dark
already	star
caught	jar
begin	arm

174

Practice Sentences

1. Nathan got a jar to catch fireflies.

2. It was already dark when he saw the first star in the sky above.

3. Soon the fireflies would begin to come out.

4. Nathan saw a light against the dark sky.

5. He caught one firefly and put it in the jar.

6. In a minute, he had five fireflies in his jar.

7. He held the jar tight with his arm and let all the fireflies out.

Fireflies
FOR NATHAN

SHULAMITH LEVEY OPPENHEIM pictures by JOHN WARD

Strategy Focus

Read Together After you read, tell what the story was about.

176

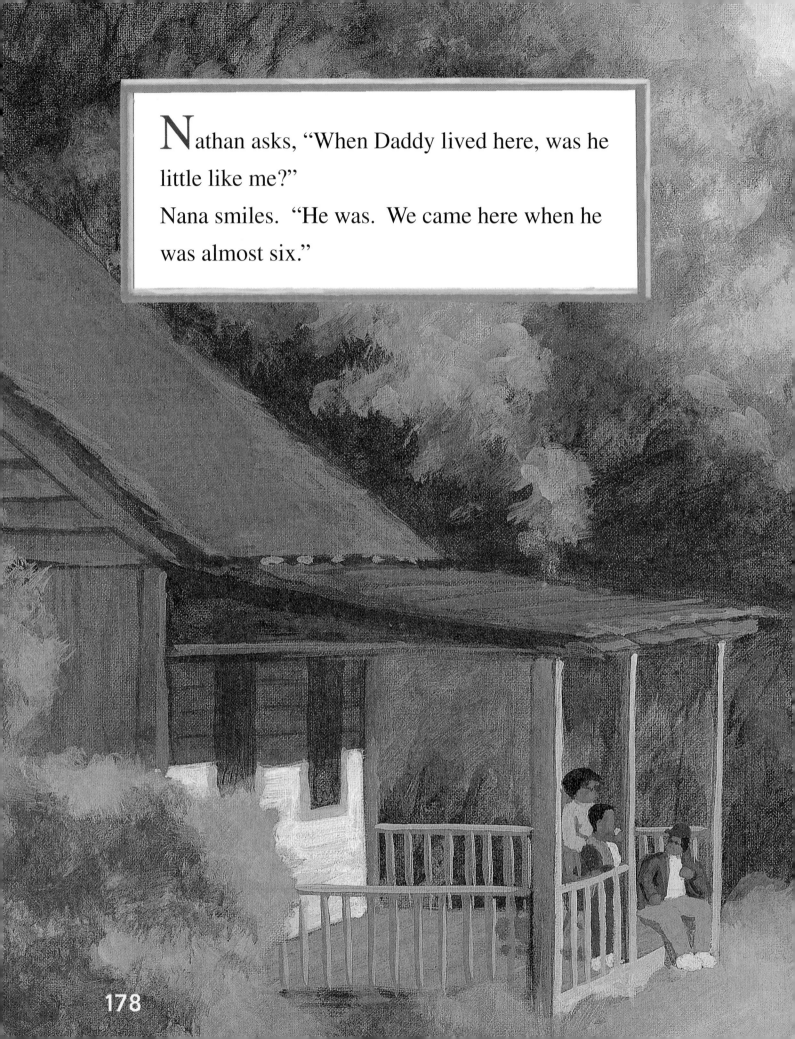

Nathan asks, "When Daddy lived here, was he little like me?"

Nana smiles. "He was. We came here when he was almost six."

178

"I'm six already," Nathan says.

"You are," and Nana kisses Nathan on the cheek.

"What was Daddy's favorite thing to do when he was six?" Nathan asks.

Nana thinks and thinks. "Fireflies," she says.

"When night came on, the three of us — your poppy, too — would creep across the lawn just when the fireflies began to star the grass. Your daddy caught a few — three, four, or five. Enough to make a shining lamp. I know exactly where the jar has been."

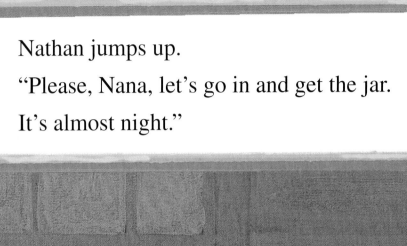

Nathan jumps up.

"Please, Nana, let's go in and get the jar.
It's almost night."

Nathan and Nana and Poppy are sitting in the grass. The sky is streaked with red. They're waiting for the night to come. Their feet are bare.

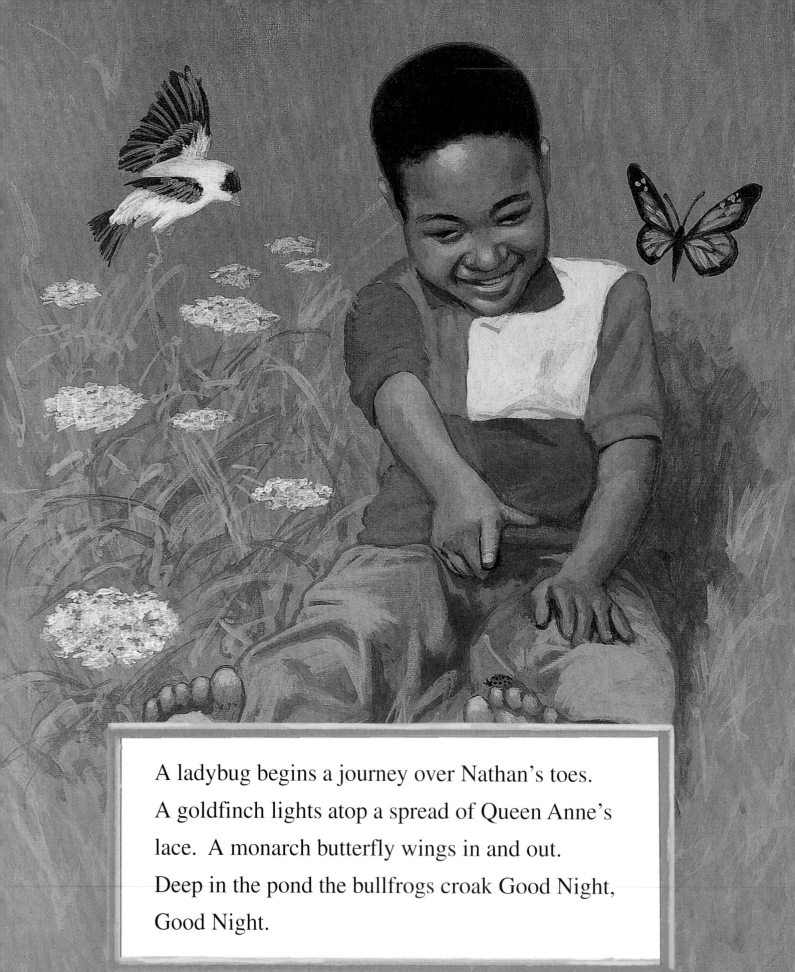

A ladybug begins a journey over Nathan's toes.
A goldfinch lights atop a spread of Queen Anne's
lace. A monarch butterfly wings in and out.
Deep in the pond the bullfrogs croak Good Night,
Good Night.

The minutes pass. Nathan shakes his leg.
The ladybug falls off his foot. He tugs at
Poppy's sleeve.

"Not yet," Poppy says.

More minutes pass. Nathan pulls at Nana's arm.

"It's getting dark. Where are the fireflies, Nana?"

"They'll be here soon."

Nana and Poppy nod their heads.

And *very* soon one, two, then three and four, the firefly glows appear. The blinking yellow lights are everywhere above the grass.

190

Nathan and Nana and Poppy creep across the lawn. "Slowly, slowly," Poppy whispers. "Let Nana hold the jar."

Nathan cups his hands around a glow.
"I've got one, Poppy! Nana, I want to see it
blinking on and off."
"Careful," Nana warns.

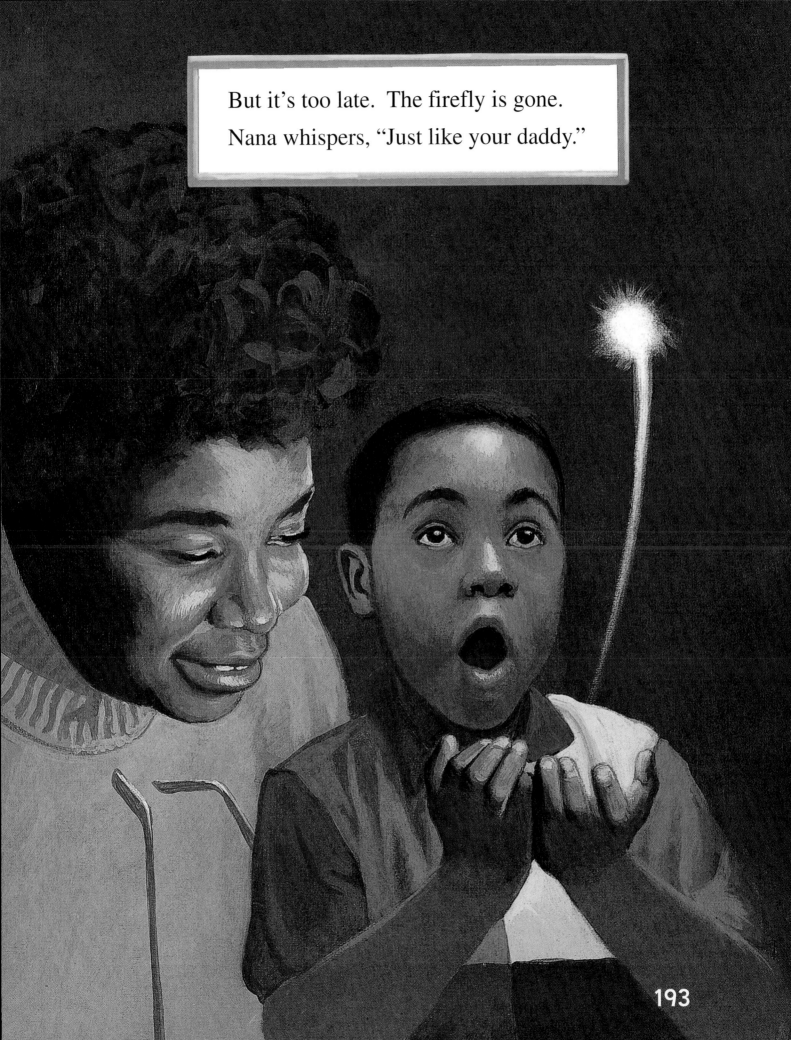

But it's too late. The firefly is gone.
Nana whispers, "Just like your daddy."

193

"You have to keep your hands cupped tightly till you drop the firefly in the jar."

Nathan promises, "I will," and soon the jar becomes a beacon in the night.

The firefly jar is sitting by the bed. Nana tucks the sheet up under Nathan's chin. Poppy kisses Nathan's cheek.

"Do you like catching fireflies with me?" Nathan asks.

"We do."

"Just as much as with my daddy?"

"Just as much."

"You can let them out when I'm asleep."

Nana and Poppy smile.

"That's what your daddy always said."

"I'm going to tell Mommy and Daddy all about catching fireflies with you."

Nathan yawns and lays the firefly jar beside him on the pillow. He presses his cheek against the glass.

"Nana, I'm glad you saved the jar."

"And so are we," Nana and Poppy tiptoe from the room. "And so are we."

Meet the Author

Besides writing books, **Shulamith Levey Oppenheim** has acted in small plays. She writes books for children and adults. She gets story ideas from spending time with her five grandchildren.

Meet the Illustrator

John Ward is an artist who lives in New York. He learned about painting in art school. His illustrations of people and families have been in many children's books.

Visit Education Place to find out more about Shulamith Levey Oppenheim and John Ward.
www.eduplace.com/kids

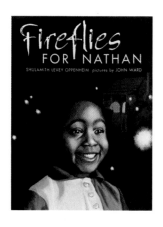

Think About the Story

1. How is Nathan like his dad?

2. Why do you think Nathan's grandparents saved the firefly jar?

3. What do you think Nathan will tell his parents about his visit?

4. Would you like to visit Nathan's grandparents? Why?

Internet

E-mail a Friend

Did you enjoy reading *Fireflies for Nathan*? Send an e-mail to tell a friend about the story.

Art

Glowing Pictures!

 1

Draw a scene from the story that shows fireflies.

 2

Use a pencil to poke holes through the fireflies on your paper.

 3

Shine a flashlight from behind your paper to make the fireflies glow!

Describing

Write a Character Sketch

Write a description about Nathan. Include details that will help someone else know what Nathan is like.

 Tips

- List words that tell what Nathan looks like and how he acts.
- Include words from your list in the sentences that you write.

Poetry Link

Read Together

Genre

Poetry

Skill: How to Read a Poem

- **Read** the title.

- **Read** the poem aloud and listen for rhyming words.

- **Think about** what the poet is comparing in the poem.

204

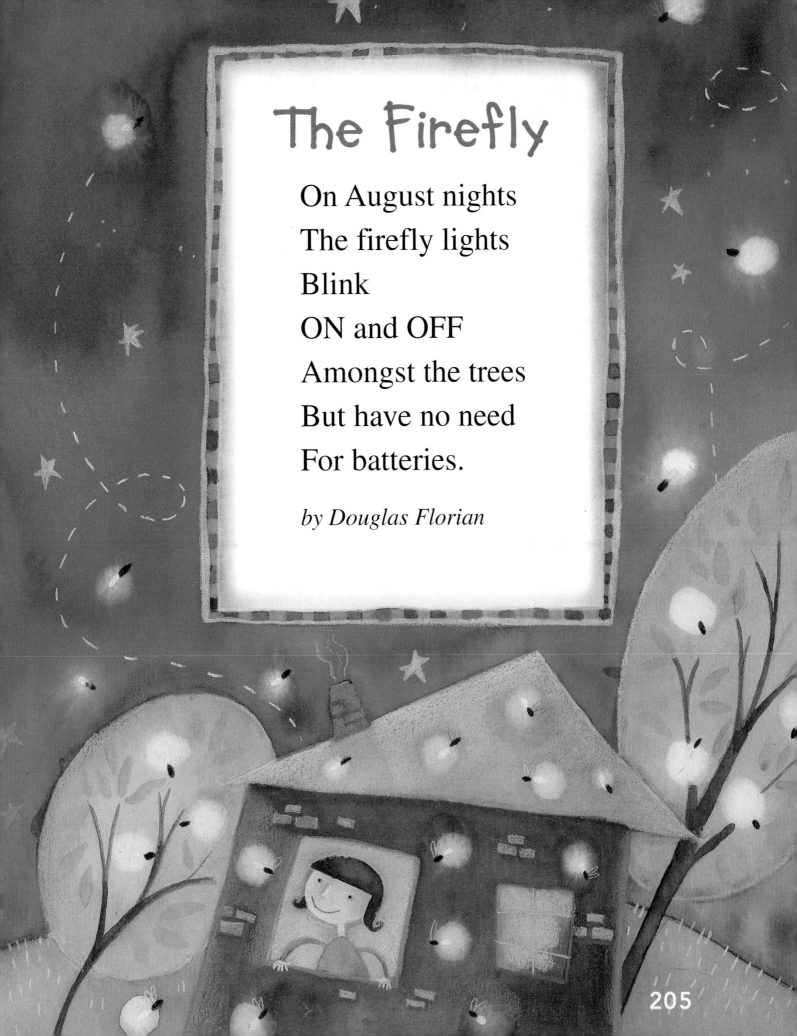

The Firefly

On August nights
The firefly lights
Blink
ON and OFF
Amongst the trees
But have no need
For batteries.

by Douglas Florian

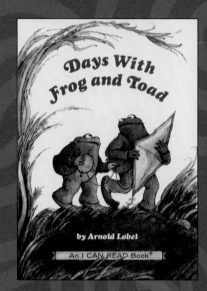

Days With Frog and Toad

by Arnold Lobel

An I CAN READ Book®

The Hat

Genre **Fantasy**

A Present for Toad

The next story is about a birthday present that's the wrong size. Discover how Frog makes the present fit.

Words to Know

able	smaller
eyes	larger
present	biggest
thoughts	

Practice Sentences

1. Frog wanted to get a present for Toad.

2. Frog had many thoughts — what if the present was a hat?

3. If the hat was smaller than Toad's head, it wouldn't fit.

4. If the hat was larger than Toad's head, it wouldn't fit.

5. If Frog got the biggest hat, it would cover Toad's eyes.

6. Would Frog be able to get the right present?

Meet the
Author and Illustrator
Arnold Lobel

Growing up, Arnold Lobel read lots of books and drew many pictures. He became an illustrator and a writer. He created more than 70 children's books. Frog and Toad are his most famous characters. Arnold Lobel got the idea from toads his children played with in Vermont.

Internet

To find out more about Arnold Lobel, visit Education Place.

www.eduplace.com/kids

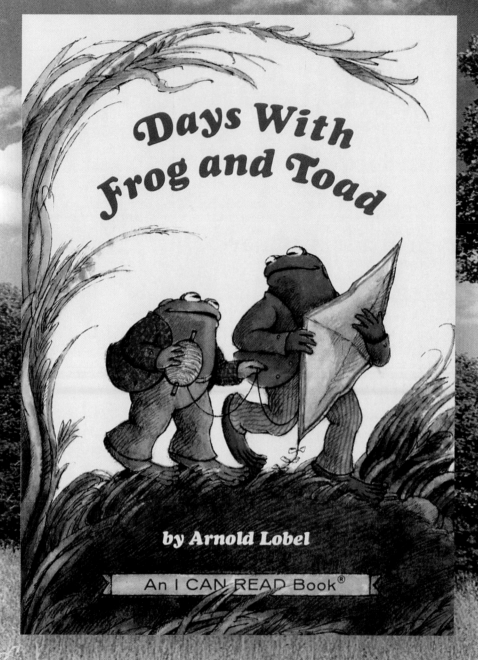

Days With Frog and Toad

by Arnold Lobel

An I CAN READ Book®

Read Together Check to make sure you understand the story as you read.

The Hat

On Toad's birthday

Frog gave him a hat.

Toad was delighted.

"Happy birthday," said Frog.

Toad put on the hat.

It fell down over his eyes.

"I am sorry," said Frog.

"That hat is much too big for you.

I will give you something else."

"No," said Toad. "This hat
is your present to me. I like it.
I will wear it the way it is."

Frog and Toad went for a walk.

Toad tripped over a rock.

He bumped into a tree.

He fell in a hole.

"Frog," said Toad,

"I can't see anything.

I will not be able to wear

your beautiful present.

This is a sad birthday for me."

Frog and Toad
were sad
for a while.
Then Frog said,

"Toad, here is what you must do.
Tonight when you go to bed
you must think
some very big thoughts.
Those big thoughts will make
your head grow larger.
In the morning
your new hat may fit."
"What a good idea," said Toad.

That night when Toad went to bed
he thought the biggest thoughts
that he could think.
Toad thought about
giant sunflowers.
He thought about tall oak trees.
He thought about high mountains
covered with snow.

Then Toad fell asleep.

Frog came into Toad's house.

He came in quietly.

Frog found the hat
and took it to his house.

Frog poured some water on the hat.

He put the hat

in a warm place to dry.

It began to shrink.

That hat grew smaller and smaller.

Frog went back to Toad's house.

Toad was still fast asleep.

Frog put the hat back on the hook
where he found it.

When Toad woke up in the morning,
he put the hat on his head.

It was just the right size.

Toad ran to Frog's house.

"Frog, Frog!" he cried.

"All those big thoughts

have made my head

much larger.

Now I can wear your present!"

Frog and Toad went for a walk.

Toad did not trip

over a rock.

He did not bump into a tree.

He did not fall

in a hole.

It turned out to be

a very pleasant

day after Toad's birthday.

Days With Frog and Toad by Arnold Lobel

Think About the Story

1. How do you know that Frog and Toad are good friends?

2. What do Frog and Toad learn in this story?

3. What would you do with a hat that would not fit?

4. Are Frog and Toad the same kind of friends the bears are in *Two Greedy Bears*?

Internet

Complete a Web Crossword Puzzle

Use words from "The Hat" to complete a crossword puzzle. Print out the puzzle from Education Place.

www.eduplace.com/kids

Science

What Shrinks?

Work with a small group to list some things that shrink. Why do you think they shrink?

Listening/Speaking

Saying Thank You

Work with a partner. Take turns being Frog and Toad. Have a conversation in which Toad thanks Frog for the birthday present.

Evaluating

Write a Book Report

Write a book report and tell what you thought of the story.

Tips

- Include the title and author.
- Write complete sentences.

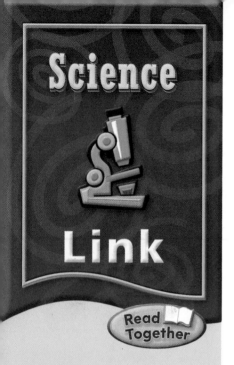
Charts

Skill: How to Read a Chart

- **Read** the headings.

- **Read** each set of facts.

- **Compare** the information.

- **Think** about what is alike and different about the facts.

Is It a Frog or a Toad?

How can you tell the difference between a frog and a toad? Read the chart and look at the pictures.

Frogs

Toads

Frogs	Toads
• Smooth, soft skin	• Thick, bumpy skin
• Long ridges down each side of back	• Short ridges on top of head
• Slender body, long legs, speedy swimmer	• Plump body, shorter legs, slower moving
• Lives in or very near water	• Lives on land, in woods
• Clumps of eggs laid in water	• Rows of eggs laid in water

Think about what you now know about frogs and toads. Look at the pictures. Can you tell which animals are frogs and which are toads?

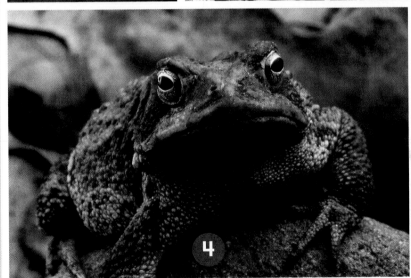

Frogs: 1, 2, 5
Toads: 3, 4

Read Together

Writing a Personal Narrative

A test may ask you to write a story about something that really happened to you. Read this sample test for *We Can Do It!*

> Write about a time when you got a present for a friend. What happened?

Tips

- Read the directions carefully. Look for key words that tell you what to write about.

- Make a plan before you write.

- Use your plan to write your story.

Here is one student's plan.

I will write about getting a present for Zach.	
Beginning Details	who the present was for big bug eyes that popped out

I need to use the words *I* and *my* in the story because this really happened to me.

I need to use details that will help the reader picture what happened.

Here is one student's answer.

Zach's Present

    I wanted to get my friend Zach a birthday present. I wanted to get him a bug book. Mom and I found the best book. It told about bugs and had big bug eyes that popped out on every page. Zach liked his book. That made me happy.

Glossary

Visit **www.eduplace.com** for
e • **Glossary** and *e* • **Word Game**.

A

appear
To **appear** means to come into view. The train will **appear** in five minutes.

appetite
Appetite means wanting food. I have a big **appetite** after I play.

argued
If you **argue** with someone, you don't agree. My brother and I **argued** about who would ride the bike.

B

beacon
A **beacon** is a light that warns people of danger. You can see the lighthouse **beacon** from miles away.

beautiful

Beautiful means very nice to look at or hear. Look at that **beautiful** painting on the wall.

bigger

Bigger means larger. That bus is **bigger** than our car.

birthday

Your **birthday** is the day you were born. We always give my mother gifts on her **birthday**.

built

To **build** is to make something. The work crew **built** a house with bricks.

C

canoe

A **canoe** is a long, thin boat. Ming used a paddle to steer the **canoe**.

cards

A **card** is a small piece of thick paper. We played a game with the **cards**.

cedar

A **cedar** is a kind of tree. We sat in the shade of the big **cedar** tree.

chicken

A **chicken** is a kind of bird. There were many **chickens** at the farm.

city

A **city** is a place where many people live and work. You can ride a bus or the subway in the **city**.

cookies

A **cookie** is a kind of food. May likes to have milk and **cookies**.

D

danger

Danger is something that can hurt you. An earthquake can put people in **danger**.

delighted

To be **delighted** means to be very happy about something. My father was **delighted** with his birthday present.

E

empty
Empty means with nothing inside. Todd drank his milk until his glass was **empty**.

equal
Equal means the same in amount or size. My father cut the sandwich into two **equal** pieces.

expected
To **expect** is to think something will happen. We **expected** the bus to be on time, but it was late.

F

favorite
Favorite means what you like the most. Spring is my **favorite** season of the year.

feathers
A **feather** is part of a bird. Most birds are covered with **feathers**.

field

A **field** is a big, flat piece of land without trees. The farmer grows hay in his **field**.

G

gathered

To **gather** means to put together. Nora **gathered** her books and put them into her backpack.

giant

Giant means much bigger than usual. The **giant** trees seemed to touch the sky.

gizzard

A **gizzard** is part of a bird's body. A bird's **gizzard** helps it break down the food it eats.

Grandaddy

Grandaddy is another name for grandfather. My **grandaddy** is my mother's father.

H

hungrier
To be **hungry** is to want to eat. I am always **hungrier** than my brother.

I

imagine
To **imagine** is to see a picture in your mind. On cold winter days, Kay likes to **imagine** that it is summer.

J

journey
A **journey** is a time when you travel somewhere. The **journey** through the mountains took many days.

L

larger
Large means big. A horse is **larger** than a dog.

M

mind

To **mind** is to care about something.
I don't **mind** if you borrow my crayons.

monarch

A **monarch** can be a kind of butterfly.
The **monarch** butterfly had beautiful
black and orange wings.

P

party

A **party** is a time when people
get together to have fun. All
my friends and family came to
my birthday **party**.

pleasant

Something that is **pleasant** makes you feel
happy. John and Rachel had a **pleasant**
day at the beach.

promises

To **promise** is to say you will do something.
Jill **promises** to be quiet during the movie.

R

remember

To **remember** is to be able to find something in your mind. Megan can **remember** all the names of the states.

S

seventh

Seventh means the one that is number seven. Anita was the **seventh** one in line.

smaller

Smaller is the opposite of bigger. A mouse is **smaller** than a horse.

soccer

Soccer is a sport you play by kicking a ball. In **soccer**, you try to kick a ball into a goal.

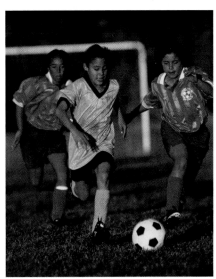

sorry

To be **sorry** is to feel sad about something. Luis was **sorry** that his friend couldn't sleep over.

stomach ache

A **stomach ache** is a pain in the belly. Keith didn't go to school because he had a **stomach ache**.

T

taught

To **teach** is to show how to do something. My sister **taught** me how to ride a bike.

thirstier

To be **thirsty** is to need a drink. The hot sun made me **thirstier**.

tired

To be **tired** is to feel weak and need rest. The long hike made Jim very **tired**.

V

vacuum cleaner

A **vacuum cleaner** is a machine that picks up dirt. I used the **vacuum cleaner** to clean the rug.

warns

To **warn** is to let someone know about danger. The reporter **warns** us if a big storm is coming.

whispers

To **whisper** is to speak in a soft voice. My mother **whispers** to me when my baby brother is asleep.

Y

years

A **year** is 365 days. Ted is seven **years** old.

Acknowledgments

For each of the selections listed below, grateful acknowledgment is made for permission to excerpt and/or reprint original or copyrighted material, as follows:

Selections

Fireflies for Nathan, by Shulamith Levey Oppenheim, illustrated by John Ward. Text copyright © 1994 by Shulamith Levey Oppenheim. Illustrations copyright © 1994 by John Ward. Reprinted by permission of HarperCollins Publishers.

Selection from *Fraction Action,* by Loreen Leedy. Copyright © 1994 by Loreen Leedy. All rights reserved. Reprinted by permission of Holiday House, Inc.

"The Hat" from *Days with Frog and Toad,* by Arnold Lobel. Copyright © 1979 by Arnold Lobel. Reprinted by permission of HarperCollins Publishers.

The New Friend, originally published as *El amigo nuevo,* by María Puncel, illustrations by Ulises Wensell. Copyright © 1995 by Laredo Publishing Company. Reprinted by permission of Laredo Publishing Company Co.

"Sister Hen's Cool Drink," retold by Angela Shelf Medearis in *A Bag of Tricks: Folk Tales from Around the World,* published by Scholastic Phonics Chapter Books. Copyright © 1998 by Scholastic Inc. Reprinted by permission. Scholastic Phonics Chapter Books is a trademark of Scholastic, Inc.

The Surprise Family, by Lynn Reiser. Copyright © 1994 by Lynn Whisnant Reiser. Reprinted by permission of HarperCollins Publishers.

Two Greedy Bears, by Mirra Ginsburg, illustrated by Jose Aruego and Ariane Dewey. Text copyright © 1976 by Mirra Ginsburg. Illustrations copyright © 1976 by Jose Aruego and Ariane Dewey. Reprinted with permission of Simon & Schuster Books for Young Readers, Simon & Schuster Children's Publishing Division.

Selection from *Watch Them Grow,* by Linda Martin. Copyright © 1994, Dorling Kindersley Limited, London. Text copyright © 1994, Linda Martin. Reprinted by permission from Dorling Kindersley.

"What Is in Mole's Sack?" retold by Gretchen Will Mayo. Copyright © 1993 by Gretchen Will Mayo. Reprinted by permission of Walker & Co.

When I Am Old with You, by Angela Johnson, illustrations by David Soman. Text copyright © 1990 by Angela Johnson. Illustrations copyright © 1990 by David Soman. Reprinted by permission of Orchard Books, New York.

Poetry

"The Firefly" from *Beast Feast,* by Douglas Florian. Copyright © 1994 by Douglas Florian. Reprinted by permission of Harcourt, Inc.

"Hope" from *Collected Poems,* by Langston Hughes. Copyright © 1994 by the Estate of Langston Hughes. Reprinted by permission of Alfred A Knopf, a Division of Random House, Inc., and Harold Ober Associates, Inc.

"I'll walk halfway to your house" from *Halfway to Your House,* by Charlotte Pomerantz. Copyright © 1993 by Charlotte Pomerantz. Reprinted by permission of HarperCollins Publishers.

"The New Girl" from *Everything Glistens and Everything Sings: New and Selected Poems,* by Charlotte Zolotow. Copyright © 1987 by Charlotte Zolotow. Reprinted with permission of Harcourt, Inc.

"A Year Later" from *The Llama Who Had No Pajama: 100 Favorite Poems,* by Mary Ann Hoberman. Copyright © 1959 by Mary Ann and Norman Hoberman. Reprinted with permission of Harcourt, Inc.

Special thanks to the following teachers whose students' compositions appear as Student Writing Models: Cheryl Claxton, Florida; Patricia Kopay, Delaware; Susana Llanes, Michigan; Joan Rubens, Delaware; Nancy Schulten, Kentucky; Linda Wallis, California

Credits